The 3T's of Ministry
Avoiding Ministry Burnout

Christopher A. Johnson Sr.

© 2014 Christopher A. Johnson, Sr.

All Rights Reserved.

No part of this publication may be reproduced, stored in a retrieval system, or transmitted, in any form or by any means, electronic, mechanical, photocopying, recording, or otherwise, without the written permission of the author.

First published by Dog Ear Publishing
4010 W. 86th Street, Ste H
Indianapolis, IN 46268
www.dogearpublishing.net

dog ear
PUBLISHING

ISBN: 978-1-4575-2988-7

Library of Congress Control Number: has been applied for

This book is printed on acid-free paper.

Printed in the United States of America

I would like to dedicate this book to my mother, Annie M. Johnson. You have instilled Values and integrity in me that have helped me Become who I am today. I love you and would like you To know that all of my success is due to your fruit of labor!

Contents

Preface .... *vii*
    Principle of Partnership
    Principle of Participation
    Principle of Progression

Introduction: Pastor Burnout 1
    What do you think about them?
    What do you think about teaching them?
    What do you think about training them?
    What do you think about trusting them?

Chapter 1: Teach Them 11
    Teach Them about Purpose
    Teach Them about Prevision
    Teach Them about Principles
    Teach Them about Passion

Chapter 2: Train Them 22
    Modeling: Model the Behavior You Seek
    Motivating: Encourage them To Launch
    Mentoring: Taking a Passive Role

Chapter 3: Trust Them 47
    Release Them: To be Followers of Christ
    Release Them: To be Fruitful for Christ
    Release Them: To be Feeders

Chapter 4: I'm Not the Senior Leader 54
    Be Teachable
    Be Trainable
    Be Trustworthy
    Bibliography

Acknowledgements

I would like to acknowledge my Lord and Savior Jesus Christ who is an inspiration to my writings. It will forever be in my heart to acknowledge my father, the late Bishop T.P. Johnson Sr., the man who taught me to be a man and gave me insight to ministry. To my wife Toya, I will forever love and honor you for your love and support. None of this would be possible if it you were not for you in my life. To the number of pastors and leaders that I have served under and with, thank you. Next, to the Mt. Zion Rucker Missionary Baptist church in Murfreesboro Tennessee and the Bethel Missionary Baptist Church in Walter Hill Tennessee, thank you for giving me experiences early in my ministry. Finally, to my beloved Zion Christian Ministries, it is a joy and a pleasure to serve as your pastor. Zion, you have made ministry worth it for me. I enjoy the partnership of advancing The Kingdom with you all.

Preface

Ministry burnout happens everywhere in the kingdom of God. It has been the cause of under achieved ministers and pastors and it is still the number one cause of unlocked potential in most of God's great men and women. It saddens me to see so many of God's servants arriving at the end of their ministry feeling empty, worthless, and unappreciated. I personally know pastors who have served for over thirty years in ministry and for some reason or another they are now at the point of giving up. I also know ministers who have tried and tried to activate their ministries in the community, but now feel as though no one cares. My heart is melted with a sense of duty for those who feel at this point in their lives that their ministries aren't going anywhere, not doing anything, and doesn't seem to be anytime soon. It is not only the seasoned pastor or ministry that has this burden. Even fresh, young, energetic, and anointed men and women seemingly want to throw in the towel because of the woes of a personally viewed ineffective ministry. Be it young or old, new or familiar, the fact still remains many of God's servants that are just burned out. They are tired from years of trying and never quite triumphing. They have been overcome by the bully of "almost". Over the years they have reached but never retained, aspired but never acquired. That will drive anyone to the point of burnout. We must ask ourselves how and why this happening to so many of our leaders is. How did we arrive at the point of burnout and why is it happening? I suggest that this happens for at least three reasons. Many of us burn out because when we look at our ministries' we lack the presence of three main principles; the principle of partnership, participation, and progression. If there aren't any partnerships, participants, or if there is a lack of progression, many ministry leaders have the propensity to burnout. This dilemma guides the etching of my pen and is what prompts me to write this book. I believe the effective practice of these three principles mentioned in this book will keep us from burning out. The following principles describe the objectives for this book; Partnership, Participation, and Progression.

Principle of Partnership

The Principle of Partnership will prove to be vital for the health and progression of any ministry. Most leaders desire others to be present in their ministries without partnering. Being present is just showing up, associating, and identifying with the ministry but not necessarily partnering. The principle of partnership promotes the idea of a mutual obligation in the ministry. It happens on two levels, one with ministers and the other with members. With ministers, we must urge them to partake with us in these ministerial labors and efforts. We must also share with them that it involves mutual perseverance and that there will be times in the ministry that they will have to endure hardships. In 2 Corinthians 8: 23, Paul calls Titus his "partner" and fellow partaker in the ministry. The word "partner" in the Greek means "sharer". Invite every minister that comes to your ministry to partner with you and share in the labor and work of God. This will give them a sense of responsibility and obligation to not spectate but become actively involved. Many of us have a "Do it all" attitude, but it is easier to realize now that you will never be able to do it all. I love what John C. Maxwell says in his book, the *17 Indisputable Laws of Leadership*, "One is Too Small a Number to Achieve Greatness" (Maxwell). I would much rather have partners in ministry than a spectator in ministry. It will be more beneficial for you to allow the ministers or pastors that connect with your ministry feel as though they are partnering with you. This kind of thinking gives them a sense of shared ownership. It moves from being just your vision to becoming "Our Vision", which means they began to birth your vision in their own lives. When something is lacking in the ministry, they will not wait for you to present the solution, they will act because they will feel the power of the partnership. Failure will not be an option to them, because a partner in the ministry will not feel as though it is you failing, but all of you will fail in their eyes. The second level of partnership happens with the members. These are the individuals that not necessarily ministers nor operate in ministry but aide in the support of the ministry. Notice Paul's partnership with the church in Philippi:

> **Philippians 4:14-16 (KJV)**
> 14 Notwithstanding ye have well done, that ye did communicate with my affliction. Now ye Philippians know also, that in the beginning of the gospel, when I departed from Macedonia, no church communicated with me as concerning giving and receiving, but ye only. 16 For even in Thessalonica ye sent once and again unto my necessity (Holy Bible, Word Search Corp.).

The partnership seems to be a cycle. Paul was dedicated to the work of the ministry and preaching the gospel. The church at Philippi understood that their way of reaching others would be to aide Paul in his ministry. They gave, and he preached. In your ministry there will be individuals that will be there for support and resourcefulness. This is the first principle we must learn to operate in.

3T Discussion:
1. What is the difference between people being present and actually partnering in the ministry?
2. What two levels will partnerships take place?
3. What are the benefits of having partners in the ministry?

3T Discovery:
Take Action: Take time this week to discover if you have partners or spectators on your team. Are you welcoming partners in the ministry?

Principle of Participation

I've never been an engineer or architect. I've never drawn a blueprint or submitted floor plan. But I can imagine that it would be very rewarding to submit some kind of plan and watch others work to bring that plan to life. What a sense of fulfillment! To gaze at the finished product would be such a reward. In ministry, you are the architect. You draw the blueprint for your ministry but you shouldn't be the only one seeing the plan. It is important for you to communicate the blueprint effectively and let those who are partnering with you become participators in the advancement of the ministry. This simply implies that you should delegate responsibility and allow those with you to participate. Too often, leaders and especially pastors have cheerleaders instead of participators. We enjoy the pump and prestige of watching other individuals cheer us on, tell us how great we are, how smart and wise we are, all to stroke our egos, but how often will we do the same for them? I am suggesting that it needs to be a team effort. Invite them to participate in the successes and the development of the ministry. They want to feel as though they have a significant role in this project. Maxwell even makes "significance" one of his indisputable laws of leadership. Listen to Maxwell the chapter of his book that deals with significance:

> "I challenge you to think of one act of genuine significance in the history of humankind that was performed by a lone human being. No matter what you name, you will find that a team of people was involved. That is why President Lyndon Johnson said, 'There are no problems we cannot solve together, and very few that we can solve by ourselves" (Maxwell).

You should have very few individuals in your ministry and especially your staff or core group that are just watching. They should all become participators. But I will share with you that they will only participate in what you allow them to participate in. Enroll and enlist them with work in mind. This is how you can ensure longevity in the ministry.

3T Discussion
1. What can you do to encourage others to participate in the ministry?
2. What do we want people to feel when they partner with the ministry?

3T Discovery
Take Action: What can you afford to release to someone else in the ministry? Find someone this week to release a task you would normally complete.

The Principle of Progression

Progress can simply be defined as the forward advancement toward perfection. In order to avoid the burnout in ministry you and I must progress our ministries. That means we must keep it moving in a direction of perfection. But how does one measure progression? That is a simple but important question which has puzzled many leaders. Many measure progression by how much money the ministry has, how many members the ministry has, how popular the ministry is, how much property the ministry has. These are all benefits or fruits from the labor but not necessarily the measure of true progression. Progression is measured by a close examination of the vision and purpose of the ministry. Always take time to assess the ministry in relation to the vision. Are we on the right track? Are we fulfilling any of our goals and objectives? Are we making steps toward where we want to be? These are all questions you should ask. When assessing progression, it does not just end at the asking of these questions but comes from making changes, updates, and improvements to the ministry IN order to get it one step closer to fulfilling the vision.

All three of these principles, if implemented and promoted in your ministry will keep you from burning out of ministry. There are unexpected turns, unforced setbacks, and difficult circumstances involved in the ministry but if you can hold these three principles close to your heart it will help guide your actions and determine the outcome of the ministry you serve in.

3T Discussion
1. What is Progression?
2. How do we measure Progression?
3. What are some questions we ask when assessing vision?

3T Discovery
Take Action: Is your ministry progressive? Are you operating in your purpose or vision? If you are and still not progressing then perhaps you should reconsider the vision and purpose of the ministry and ask God for fresh insight.

INTRODUCTION
My Good Friend, Pastor Burnout

I would like to introduce you to my friend Pastor Burnout. I refer to him this way because I want him to remain anonymous. He has been a great friend and mentor to me and I praise God for him but he has reached the point of burnout in his ministry. This pastor has served for more than thirty years in the ministry, he has baptized hundreds of people, led hundreds to Christ, seen more than fifty ministers come and go from his ministry, and now as he glances back over the years and looks comparatively at his ministry now, and admittedly he is burned out! But alarmingly when he reflects about the ministry and its past failures, broken relationships, and unfulfilled goals, none of it is his fault. Pastor burnout has not taken responsibility or ownership of any of the issues. Every minister or leader that has left the ministry has done so upset and angry at him. Every member that has moved on has done so because of the approach to leadership and ministry that he seems to take. Yet, Pastor Burnout seems to think there is no need for him to change because after all it is their fault. He shouts accusations such as, "They will not listen to me", "I don't trust them", "they will not do what I ask them", "they are just trying to take over", "they aren't ready to lead yet", "and I am the Pastor"! These are all examples of what Pastor Burnout would say. But none of these stated frustrations have anything to say about what he could have done differently or more effectively as a leader. It was everyone else's fault as if he had no role to play in the situation. In your ministry, you must always look at things from a personal note first. What could I have done better? Did I prepare the individual for their task? Did I show them how I wanted it done? A personal assessment should always be performed initially. As I responded to Pastor Burnout, I knew that nothing I said could fix the relationships with his departed ministers and leaders and nothing I could have done would heal his dilemma. However, I could plant a seed of consideration into his thinking. Allow me this opportunity to share with you three questions I asked to my friend, "Pastor Burnout".

What do you think about them?

What you think about people and your perception of them will have a great deal to do with how you treat them. Individuals that you see in a negative light, you will naturally mistreat them. If you have a positive perception of someone, you will in turn handle them with care. It is important that you maintain a positive perception of everyone that partners with your ministry. Even if the individual has mistreated you, you must always stay focused on the matters at hand and realize that "we wrestle not against flesh and blood". Your perception of them must remain consistently positive. When you see everyone in this light then you will guard yourself against treating anyone with contempt or disrespect. Listen to the apostle Paul as he really sheds light on this issue:

> **Titus 1:15 (KJV)** [15] Unto the pure all things *are* pure: but unto them that are defiled and unbelieving *is* nothing pure; but even their mind and conscience is defiled. (Holy Bible, Word Search Corp.)

> **Philippians 4:8 (KJV)**
> [8] Finally, brethren, whatsoever things are true, whatsoever things *are* honest, whatsoever things *are* just, whatsoever things *are* pure, whatsoever things *are* lovely, whatsoever things *are* of good report; if *there be* any virtue, and if *there be* any praise, think on these things. (Holy Bible, Word Search Corp.)

As it relates to those who will partner with you on a daily basis the question becomes, which lens will you look out of today? Will you look through a defiled lens, or will you look out a pure lens? John C. Maxwell says, "One of the reasons people don't achieve their dreams is that they desire to change their results without changing their thinking" (Maxwell, Thinking for A Change) More than likely, many pastors or leaders mistreat those partnering with them because of a negative perception they may have of them which doesn't reflect the reality that person's character or intent. If you think they are against you then you will treat them that way. If you think they don't like you then you will treat them that way as well. The truth is that you need those individual to bring success to your ministry. Treat them that way! They are a missing ingredient in your unfinished project! You must garner this new way of thinking in order to make your ministry effectively burnout free! Treat everyone like you need them to make this collective effort a success. "Look at it this way: an executive depends on people to carry out his instructions. If they don't, the company president will fire the executive, not the employees. A salesman depends on people to buy his product. If they don't, the salesman fails. Likewise, a college dean depends on professors to carry forward his educational program; a politician depends on voters to elect him; a writer depends on people to read what he writes…. Today remember, a person either supports you willingly or he doesn't support you at all". (Schwartz) As I ministered to Pastor Burnout that day, I wanted him to really get a grasp on what he could have done to begin to change the way he viewed or thought about those who were partnering with him. I submitted to him at least 10 ways in which he could do that according to a method developed by President Lyndon Johnson even before he became the president. Consider the following:

1. Learn to remember names. Inefficiency at this point may indicate that your interest is not sufficiently outgoing.
2. Be a comfortable person so there is no strain in being with you. Be an old-shoe, old-hat kind of individual.

3. Acquire the quality of relaxed easy-going so that things do not ruffle you.
4. Don't be egotistical. Guard against the impression that you know it all.
5. Cultivate the quality of being interesting so people will get something of value from their association with you.
6. Study to get the "scratchy" elements out of your personality, even those of which you may be unconscious.
7. Sincerely attempt to heal, on an honest Christian basis, every misunderstanding you have had or now have. Drain off your grievances.
8. Practice liking people until you learn to do so genuinely.
9. Never miss an opportunity to say a word of congratulation upon anyone's achievement, or express sympathy in sorrow or disappointment.
10. Give spiritual strength to people, and they will give genuine affection to you.

(Schwartz)

I urged my dear pastor friend in the same way that I am urging you right now to begin to think of the people around you in a different manner. See the potential in them rather than the flaws in them. This will lead to you treated them better and keeping a relationship with them that will last and survive the test of time.

What do you think about teaching them?

"Teaching them? I do teach them! They have been under my teaching for years" exclaimed Pastor Burnout. "They have been getting good solid teaching under my tutelage," he said. Well, that is not the issue then. We can agree that you have provided teaching over the years. I will give the good pastor that. But there are two very important questions that must be asked in all of the teaching as we examine the problem at hand. Even though you are and have been teaching, is learning still taking place? Next, what are you teaching? I have often said that regardless if you consider yourself a profound and prolific teacher or not, the true measure of successful teaching is whether or not the student has learned. If learning has taken place then in my opinion, that is great teaching. If the learning has in some way ceased then there is an issue between the teaching and the learning that we must deal with. There is a barrier between the teacher and the student. If someone partnering in your ministry has stopped learning from you then there is something hindering their learning capacity. In essence, the student must feel a connection to the teacher. "Some teachers focus on the content they desire to cover in the class as the primary factor in teaching. Creative Bible teachers do not. They recognize the necessity of teaching the truth of the Bible and the importance of strong content, but they also know that they teach students, not lessons. Student's needs and student learning are priority. Creative Bible teachers see themselves as a link between the content and the student. By knowing and caring for their students, they are able to connect the content in meaningful ways with students' lives. Needs assessment helps teachers do this". (Bredfeldt) Many things can hinder the students learning. How valuable they feel to the ministry, how confident they are, how they feel about you and your teaching, how you treat them, and how often they are able to hear or receive your teaching. These are all factors that may hinder the students learning. Over the years in ministry, we must all assess the students and evaluate the rate in which they are learning. We must also assess if they are learning at all. This requires us to take time with them, meet with them, test them, ensure their progress and continue to provoke a learning spirit within them. Many students or ministers will reach a point to where they feel as though they have plateaued under your ministry. At that point, it is time for them to step out with your blessing to begin to teach. The reason why so many pastors have friction with associate ministers or assistant ministers is they feel as though they are "just not getting it". Could it be perhaps that they have gotten years ago but now they are just ready to move on to something else? This is important. Ask yourself this question, are they learning? If the answer to that is no, be very careful because if they are not then they will not be with you very long. If the answer is yes, then that will bring us to our next question to ask under the whole teaching issue.

The next question is "What am I teaching?" I must say that if what you are teaching is self-serving and totally doctrinal then you will eventually find yourself like Pastor Burnout. Most leaders teach but they only teach things that seem to be beneficial to them. For example, Pastor Burnout even now is teaching a class on "The Protocols of the Pastor" which tells members how to properly treat and carry themselves around the senior pastor. The problem with that is there are so many other areas that need attention. The members are not motivated, there are no true objectives for the ministry, there's no clear-cut vision for the ministry. Based upon these facts, I hardly think that the protocols of the pastor are top priority. If what is being taught is self-centered, those supporting or partnering with you will automatically shut you off because there is another student need that is not being met. Try and avoid being self-serving in your teaching. Next, try to avoid teaching doctrine. Doctrinal opinions will vary and the reality is not everyone will agree with your doctrinal position. Most people have real deep doctrinal positions but will still support and partner with you even if you differ. Never focus on teaching doctrine. Remember, you can win a doctrinal argument and lose a dangling soul. Frustrated and convicted Pastor Burnout shouted, "Well what am I supposed to teach then?" This is a question that we will answer in this book. Regardless of the content, and taking into consideration these questions, we still should "Teach them".

3T Discussion
1. What are you teaching your ministry leaders about your vision and purpose?
2. Do you feel as though everyone is learning and retaining the information?
3. Are their flaws in your leadership dynamic that is hindering learning for the students?

3T Discovery
Take Action: Take time this week to teach at least three aspects of the vision that you don't share with most people. God has given you insight that no one else has.

What do you think About Training Them?

As expected, my dear friend thought that he was in essence providing the training that was necessary for his ministers over the years. The truth is that he probably was providing training but it was his own perception of it. I will deal with training in more detail later in this book but many leaders often make the mistake of training others on their terms instead of assessing the needs and fears of others. I would love to think of training in relation to the word "opportunity". This is a constant progression in ministry. After you have taught them, it is necessary to train them. With all of the instruction that you have given your ministers and leaders need opportunity to exercise learned information. This will act as a sign that true learning has taken place and it gives them training in the specified area. Let me give a few examples:

1. Teaching a class on homiletics would be an example of teaching. Giving them the opportunity to preach is the training.
2. Teaching a class on love is an example of teaching. Giving them opportunity to express the love is training.
3. Teaching a class serving is an example of teaching. Giving them the opportunity to serve is the training.

In every case, teaching should be coupled with training. Provide them with opportunities to teach, preach, serve, plan, oversee, and operate the ministry. This will allow them to practice what they have been taught plus give a certain level of experience. This kind of training also gives you an opportunity to correct, exhort, and instruct. Eventually each minister who is being trained will be able to operate in the spirit of excellence that God has given to you. This allows you to focus on other areas and not have to micromanage in ministry because you know that you have trained effectively. I shared with Pastor Burnout that the opportunities we provide for them today will one day become their reality. I often share with the ministers that come to partner with us that as they accept their call into the ministry that they are discovering a gift as a rookie soldier does his new weapon. It seems unfamiliar and frightening at first. Before the young cadet holds it in his or her hands they have to learn about it. There is a class given to them concerning how the gun works, its limitations, its features, etc. It is not until the young soldier puts the gun in his hands that he begins to become familiar with the weaponry. In a like manner, those who are partnering with you have a gift that they are not familiar with and they are clueless as how to use it. As their leaders we must provide them with the training to show them how to use the gift. The next time God sends gifted, talented, and assertive individuals train them!

3T Discussion
1. What is the difference between teaching and training?
2. When training is provided, it gives the trainee _____.

3T Discovery
Examine your structure in your ministry. What training modules do you have in place? Can one be developed in your ministry? Have you provided any opportunities in the ministry?

What Do You Think About Trusting Them?

My friend Pastor Burnout had the most trouble with the next question I asked him. I asked him, "What do you think about trusting them?" He looked offended. He felt protective of something as if someone was trying to take everything he had worked for. He acted as if the pastor thirty years of ministry was under attack and someone was trying to lay hold of the seeds that he has sown. He said, "Trust them with what"? "No", he said. "I don't trust any of them; they don't know what they are doing". Well, I submitted to him that they would not know what they are doing if you don't show them what to do. Most of us will not trust individuals that we feel are rebellious, inadequate, under qualified. If they are rebellious it is probably because we have not taken the time to teach them or train them. This leads to a lack of trust. The point I was trying to convey to the good pastor was that if you have taught them, if you have trained them, why not trust them. Even if you don't trust them, trust the time, energy, and deposits you have given them. Let us look deeper into these three practices that will eventually cause you to prevent the burnout of ministry. Teach Them, Train Them, and Trust Them! That was my petition to him that day so let us take this journey together.

3T Discussion
1. Do you have trust issues? Do you have any issues letting go of something and letting someone else take ownership of it?

3T Discovery
Take time to reflect on the individual that has spent the most time in your ministry or a lot of time in your ministry. You can have a sub-par relationship or very good one. Do you trust them? Before you answer begin to think about the investments that you have made into their lives. If you don't trust them, can you bring yourself to trust what you have deposited?

CHAPTER 1

Teach Them

One of the most difficult things to do in ministry is to persuade people to become committed to your ministry day after day and month after month. If reaching for the principle of participation is your aim, you will have to have the power of influence. As a leader, it will take a bit of convincing on your part in order to prompt participation in this effort. "Leadership is a process of influence. Anytime you seek to influence the thinking, behavior, or development of people toward accomplishing a goal in their personal or professional lives, you are taking on the role of a leader" (Hodges). A leader must teach. Teaching is a vital part of influence. If you are seeking to lead without teaching you will have a tough time at that. I want to submit to you what will prove to be important things to teach those who will follow you in your ministry. Regardless of how big or small your ministry is these areas of teaching should be a central part of how you approach the operation of the ministry. Remember, as you teach each individual about aspects of your ministry they will begin to see the importance of each lesson in their own ministry. By teaching them how you administrate, they learn that administration is important. By teaching them about your purpose, previsions, principles, and passions they understand that these things are important. Let us look at what we are to teach them a little closer.

Teach Them about Purpose

I've often told those in my ministry that the fundamental question we must ask is "why are we here"? The answer to that question is what defines the purpose. The purpose is the driving force of the ministry; it is what urges commitment in tough and trying times. When individuals seemingly want to quit, the purpose statement keeps them engaged. No one was greater at identifying their purpose than Jesus Christ. He freely communicated why he was here in several passages of scripture. Note these particular passages:

Matthew 15:24 (KJV)
But he answered and said, I am not sent but unto the lost sheep of the house of Israel.

Matthew 18:11 (KJV)
For the Son of man is come to save that which was lost.

Luke 19:9-10 (KJV)
And Jesus said unto him, this day is salvation come to this house, forasmuch, as he also is a son of Abraham. For the Son of man is come to seek and to save that which was lost.

It is quite clear that Christ knew his purpose and he had no problem communicating the purpose to his followers. He did not come for individuals who had it all together, but his purpose for coming was clearly communicated. Christ came to seek and to save those which are lost. In a like manner we must be willing to teach about purpose in general but also to teach our purpose. Remember, by teaching them your purpose it has a triple benefit. They will begin to partner with you and participate with you, but also be motivated to progress you! Tell them why you are in ministry. Tell them why you have stepped out on faith. Let them know your heart. People tend to partner with individuals they know a little bit more about. I love how Ken Blanchard addresses communicating purpose in his book entitled *Lead like Jesus*:

What business are you in? What are you trying to accomplish? What is your mission statement? Jesus was clear about what business He and His disciples were in. He called His disciples, not just to become fishermen but to a greater purpose—to become "fishers of men" (Matthew 4:19). An effective mission statement should express a higher purpose for the greatest good that gives meaning to the efforts of each individual involved in your organization….A clear purpose sets the direction for where you are going. At the Lead like Jesus ministry, our purpose is "to inspire and equip people to lead like Jesus to restore joy to work and family." As we have continually emphasized, without clear direction, leadership doesn't matter. (Hodges)

In our ministry, communicating to those partnering with us the reason why we preach, teach, minister, etc. is of great importance. It reduces the frustrations of upsets and under achievements. Purpose initiates the drive needed to endure hardships and trials. I can imagine that Jesus kept his purpose on his mind his whole ministry. His purpose was to seek and to save. Through all of the doubters and discouragers, seek and save. Through all of the pains pressures of the cross, seek and save. No matter what the test was, Jesus' purpose energized his actions. Why didn't he come down off the cross? He was the Son of God and he could have delivered himself and saved the others as well. What made him endure? What committed him to the dogwood tree? Why did he choose the nails? I submit that his purpose nailed him to the cross, and kept him there. One nail said "seek", the other "save", the other nail through his feet "the lost". There will be no trial that you are faced with in your ministry that will destroy your ministerial effort if you teach purpose to your ministers. When there is no money being made, they understand "that's not our purpose", when there is no red carpet being unrolled, "that's not our purpose", those things will not drive us but we will be driven by purpose. By teaching them your purpose you will help them discover the meaning for their own ministry. What a great way to keep them sparked and motivated, Teach Them about Purpose!

Teach Them about Prevision

At Zion Christian Ministries, which is the name of the ministry God has placed me over, we have learned that focusing on the future is always more beneficial than focusing on where you are at. When we first begun our ministry, we were meeting in a theatre on a college campus. After four months, we moved from the theatre to a funeral chapel which is our current location. It would have been easy for us to become discourage and begin to crumble under the pressure of uncertainty, but God kept ringing the word "vision" in my head. We had a vision and God had already given a prevision of what our future would look like. That was our focus. Whenever your ministry is empowered behind the vision, your current situation has no bearing on the progression of the ministry because that is not what they will focus on. They will always be excited about where they are going, not where they are at. By making previsions I mean that you develop a clear picture of your future and communicate it to the team. My friend Pastor Burnout could have salvaged many of the broken relationships in his ministry if he would have pushed the vision a little more. What I have discovered is that you can have a ministry with dynamic preaching, awesome teaching, and curriculum can be second to none but when it comes to the progression of the ministry and the participation in the ministry you're lacking in those areas. Why? Well a better question is, "What are they participating in? And what are they progressing to? This is where your vision comes in. It really gives everyone something to focus on. Vision is the road map so to speak. It is the "big picture" of the puzzle. It is what the ministry is supposed to ultimately look like. Teaching them your vision is vitally important because they will always know the expectation and strive to focus on that. John Maxwell in his book *Talent is Never Enough* eludes effects of focus and vision in an individual. He says, "If you desire to achieve something, you first need to know what your target is. That's true even when it comes to personal development. If you lack focus, you will be all over the place. Attempting everything, like attempting nothing, will suck the life out of you. It will sap you of energy and new opportunities. And whatever momentum you have going for you will be diminished" (Maxwell, Talent is Never Enough Workbook).

Promoting the big picture is going to benefit the ministry in more ways than you think. When you dedicate time to teach them your vision you are basically giving them the finished product and telling them this is what I'm looking for. This helps them work toward bringing fulfillment to the vision but also teaches them that they are to become visionaries as well. Vision focuses their thinking. Maxwell quoting Alvin Toffler says, "You've got to think about 'big things' while you're doing small things, so that the small things go in the right direction" (Maxwell, Thinking for A Change). What an awesome truth. The big things should direct the small things. What you are doing now will have an effect on the big picture. What you teach them now will have an effect on the big picture. Listen to Maxwell again:

> Have you ever heard the expression, "We'll cross that bridge when we come to it"? This expression was more than likely written by someone who didn't see the big picture. The world was built by people who "crossed bridges" in their minds long before anyone else did. The only way to break new ground or move into uncharted territory is to move beyond the immediate and see the big picture (Maxwell, Thinking for A Change).

The bible has much to say about communicating vision as well. Listen to what God tells Habakkuk to do concerning vision:

Habakkuk 2:2 (KJV)
And the LORD answered me, and said, Write the vision, and make *it* plain upon tables, that he may run that readeth it.

There are several dynamics to consider from this passage of scripture. Notice how God instructs the prophet to communicate the vision. He says to him write it down. In other words, put it in a statement form. Then he says to him "make it plain". Make the vision understandable to the recipients. That is why you must teach it to them and insure that they have a clear understanding of it. This will result in them being motivated to run when they read it. As I reflect over Pastor Burnout's conversation, I remember him sharing with me the fact that they would often carry things out that he did not desire to happen. This was a result of not effectively communicating what he did want to happen. He didn't communicate his vision! If you want them to do it right, if you want them to do it the way you want it done, the solution is quite simple, teach them about Prevision!

Teach Them about Principles

A principle is a defined as a fundamental truth, law, or doctrine. It is a motivating source. Principles often determine an individual's behavior. I've mentioned in some of my other works what I share with every leader that partners with our ministry the importance of principles. I try to let them know as often as I can that they are to be Christian first, then whatever title they are. Paul was an apostle, missionary, and pastor but at the core of all of this he was simply a Christian. Although there are many principles that are important to cover I believe that three really stand out and are important to teach. Make sure that when you teach those who partner with you about principles that you teach them the principle of Flexibility, Accountability, and Teachability.

Flexibility is not conformity, there is a major difference. To be flexible is to learn to stretch to heights or depths that are against the norm. It promotes the whole idea of adaptability and open-mindedness. However, conformity is different in the sense that when you conform to something you began to take the shape of something or become what your environment is. One of the things we have to teach to partnering ministers or leaders is that it is dangerous to conform but we must be flexible. We shouldn't conform because our environments change too much. Not every plan will be executed perfectly, not every dream will be fulfilled quickly, and not every day will flow smoothly. In saying this, we must all learn to be flexible. Most of our discouragement comes when we expect every detail in our lives to go as we planned them. When it doesn't, we tend to think that there is something hindering us or that we are operating outside of what God has called us to do. We have to be flexible enough to make the best of all of our bad situations. I love the attitude Paul apparently takes in Philippians 1:13 when on house arrest in chains he declares, "The things which have happened to me have fallen out rather for the furtherance of the gospel". In all of our surprises, setbacks, our sidetracks we must remain flexible. We can lose our composure but remain cool. Flexibility allows room for disappointments. Remember what Paul says in Philippians 4: 11-12, "Not that I speak in respect of want: for I have learned, in whatsoever state I am, *therewith* to be content. I know both how to be abased, and I know how to abound: everywhere and in all things I am instructed both to be full and to be hungry, both to abound and to suffer need" (Holy Bible, Word Search Corp.). This describes the true meaning of being flexible. Allow for bad days, good days, and for average days because they will come. What we must remember in all of these situations is that there are times where we just have to go with the flow. Imagine what Abraham's day would have been like if God didn't provide a ram in the bush for him on the top of Mount Sinai. His commandment was to go offer up his son as a sacrifice, but just when he was ready to do so, God switched his plans. Abraham stopped what he was doing and went a totally different direction. That is flexibility. Teach everyone that partners with your ministry to be flexible. This kind of thinking will reduce a great deal of stress.

"Superior leaders seek to surround themselves with an accountability system that helps them avoid character failure. This practice in and of itself is a sign of strength versus weakness. A major character flaw is to believe oneself to be above failure and immune to the temptations other leaders face" (Toler). Accountability comes with the job. All of us who are leaders have to be accountable. We cannot ask others to uphold principles and standards that we do not practice. We have a personal, public, and penal responsibility that we must uphold. Personally all of us should desire to do what is right in the sight of God and all of those who follow us. This translates to mean that there are just certain things that Christians just shouldn't do. There should be an inner conviction to do what is holy and righteous in the sight God. Many of us have become good and covering up our sin and learning how to coat the outward sin, but if you are to teach them anything, teach them to deal with the inner sin and that is what the bible refers to as iniquity. In Psalms 66: 18 it reads *"If I regard iniquity in my heart, the Lord will not hear me"* (Holy Bible, Word Search Corp.). Wow! God will not even hear our prayers until we deal with the inner sin. This kind of teaching does not happen anymore as often as it should in the house of God. These are principles you should live by and also teach to your leaders. Remember to teach them that salvation is an inside out thing and if we are to walk it out properly it must stem from an inner integrity. Before you teach them to preach, teach, administrate, or perform remember lesson number one, "Personal Accountability". There is also a public accountability that we must fall in submission to. In other words, there is a conviction that falls over me if I feel like someone else may observe my sin. It his healthy for all of us in leadership to fill this way and public accountability should keep us from living unrighteous lives. Paul gives credence to this way of thinking in 2 Corinthians 3:2, *"Ye are our epistle written in our hearts, known and read of all men"* (Holy Bible, Word Search Corp.). In other words, all of us are walking epistles and men and women are reading our lives. The question is "What are they reading"? Can it be said that all of us are walking worthy of the call of God before others. This is all a part of our public accountability to each other. There are certain behaviors I will not entertain because I know my two sons and baby daughter are watching me. That is a public accountability that should be present in us all. Think of the error many young Christians may fall into if they are observing this kind of living in their leaders. If we are not careful we will raise a generation of believers that really don't know God nor seeks to please him. Teach them to live right, live holy, and be a person of integrity after all someone may be watching. Lastly, there is a penal standard that we must uphold and remain accountable to. This means that there are consequences to the sin that we engage in. We all must realize that as leaders we have to be accountable to the punishments that we hold so strictly with others. My friend pastor burnout didn't realize that most of the people who partnered with his ministry had lost a level of respect for him because he would expect things from them that he wouldn't hold himself accountable to. This kind of hypocritical leadership only scars the ministry and his reputation. All of us who have been given the privilege to serve God's people in leadership must be true to the office, true to ourselves, and most of all true to God. There are some things that must not be sacrificed and Godly principles should top the list for any leader enrolled in God's army.

Teach Them about Passion

One can only but imagine the scene on Calvary centuries ago when a man hung on a tree for sins that he didn't commit. The pain from the torture must have dismantled his will, crushed his strength, and drained him of the eagerness to go on. Why? That is the question I asked! The question should not be why didn't he stay down, but why did he get up? Why did he rise after every beat down, every blow, and every attack? He never questioned his accusers but he endured, he persisted. Why? I believe it can be summed up in the Title that Mel Gibson uses to depict the last few hours of the life of Jesus Christ. It was not his muscular frame that drove him to be 'obedient even unto death'. It was not his charisma, fame, nor prominence. It was indeed the Passion of Christ that held the nails in his hands, and drove the peg through his feet. It was Passion! I love the way the word is described in the Greek language "to *experience* a sensation or impression (usually painful) feel, passion, suffer (Word Search). What an awesome depiction! To be passionate about something simply means that it grieves you to think of its trodden condition. It can cause you to cry, feel pain, or sometimes cause you to reject it. When you are passionate about something, no matter how tough it gets you always find a way to it and through it. The most difficult thing to process is that often what we are the most passionate about is what we are most irritated by. However, no matter what the situation may be passion always keeps you centered and driven. I believe that as we are pouring into these people who will partner with us that we must teach them to be passionate. There are three circles of passion that may help ground our emotions and give guidance to our feelings. First we must be passionate about people, then passionate about productivity, and finally passionate for potential.

It is impossible in my opinion, to be successful in ministry and have little or no passion for people. There should be a burning desire in all of us in ministry as leaders to see people grow. Out of our deep passion to see that our ministry becomes one hinged on love and genuine care for people. Even though we should possess that love for people we must remember that what we are passionate about can also be our biggest disappointments but because we are passionate about people we find a way to look beyond faults and see needs. Jeremiah the Prophet of God gives us a great example of this because his passion was closely tied to his people. Notice his dilemma in the following verses, "I wish that my head were filled with water and my eyes were a fountain of tears so that I could cry day and night for my dear people who have been killed" (Jeremiah 9:1) In almost the same breath, he communicates to us his disgust and disappointment with the people, "I wish I had a place to stay in the desert. I would abandon my people and go away from them. They are all adulterers, a mob of traitors." (Jeremiah 9:2) Jeremiah is caught between what Dr. Robert Smith Jr. calls "two inescapable extremes". Jeremiah is between 'I can't go on, but I can't give up'. What keeps you? How do you continue in the fight when you are warring between these two? The answer is quite simple for Jeremiah he says it like this, "I think to myself, I can forget the Lord and no longer speak his name. But his Word is inside me like a burning fire shut up in my bones. I wear myself out holding it in, but I can't do it any longer." (Jeremiah 20:9) Plainly seen is the fact that if you are passionate about something it burns inside you to the point that you cannot hold it in. Passion will cause you to press on even when you feel like giving up. Many ministry leaders today are not driven by passion. We are driven by cars, money, building projects, and worldly status. God requires of us to be passionate about what we do. We should have a heart-felt desire to see people saved, developed, and achievers. That should be what we are passionate about. Teach this; drive the point home because it will always put ministry in perspective for your followers. Passion is so tied to emotion that it can overwhelm us but I believe that it is healthy to instill passion into your leaders. It humbles us, it guides us, and it also focuses us. Right now my young boys are very involved in sports. My oldest son, C.J., is very passionate about basketball. It is evident because he has great displeasure in losing. He is overcome by tears when he loses even at this young age. However, what I love to see is that because he is passionate about it, he discovers why the team lost and he will work harder at those things in practice. This kind of thinking can also be applied to ministry. Learn what things are weaknesses and began to develop them. Don't marinate in your misery but allow that passion to drive you to get better. In ministry there will be pitfalls and there will be bumps in the middle of the road along the way. Allow passion to be the pilot that keeps you and your team in the middle of the road. "Clearly one of the major functions of the rural preacher is to be an educator. I am not thinking of the fact that good preaching always has teaching values, or of the fact that the greatest of all preachers was "a teacher come from God". (Hewitt) Of all the many things you must teach, please remember to teach on passion!

3T Discussion
1. Name three things that you can teach them.
2. What is Passion?
3. What is Prevision?
4. What are principles?

3T Discovery
You must teach! There is no other way around it. What is hindering you from being the teacher in your ministry? You should be the "master" teacher in your ministry.

CHAPTER 2

Train Them

It is by no coincidence that Proverbs 22:6 says "Train up a child in the way they should go" and not "Teach" the child in the way they should go. Training, as we mentioned earlier is a tad bit different from teaching. In both cases learning is taking place but with the training aspect there is a more practical hands on dynamic. The Hebrew word used in this scripture means to discipline, to dedicate, or to demonstrate. It took me a while to understand this whole concept until I had children of my own. Training is much more in-depth than teaching. For example, I taught my son Jerell how to ride a bike and the first thing I did was teach him about the bike. These are the handlebars, this is the seat, these are the wheels, these are the pedals, etc. That was teaching. But now sooner or later he had to ride for himself and that would require me to apply the "training" wheels. Notice the function of the training wheels. They are to assist the rider by maintaining balance and to ensure that rider gains confidence and comfort until the rider can ride unassisted. In a like manner, we are to use training for the same function. We are provide training for them ride their spiritual bikes until the training gives them confidence to ride on their own. One of the biggest mistakes many leaders make is they allow underdeveloped ministers or team members to sit on the staff without training them or challenging them to become better. This will only produce complacent mindsets in your ministry. Telling them what to do is just the beginning, showing them what to do is the next step, and allowing them to practice it will gradually initiate growth and development. In the previous chapter we expressed the importance of teaching. This chapter will deal primarily with training those who partner with your team. There are three major components of training that I will isolate in this chapter. If we are to train effectively we must practice modeling, motivating, and mentoring. Clear your mind and analyze your approach carefully. By the end of this chapter, ask yourself if you are the best trainer you can be. Remember, you can never expect of them what you haven't put in them. If you did not train them, never expect them to act, respond, or be like you. Every minister, leader, or person that comes under your auspices is and will only be a product of your training. If you have done so effectively it will show, if you haven't it will show as well. I believe that by now you know the urgency to teach them so let's take it a step further, Train Them!

Modeling: Model the Behavior You Seek

We practice this whole concept of modeling more often than we think. I remember vividly teaching my son how to take his first jump shot. After telling him how he should do it for thirty minutes I finally grabbed the ball myself and said "look son, like this!" In order for him to really catch the concept I had to model the form and technique that I was looking for. In a like manner as leaders we must be models of the kind of behavior that we are seeking from our leaders. Let them see you giving then you can challenge them to give! Let them see you loving then you can challenge them to love! Let them see your commitment then you can challenge their commitment. In all things, you must model the behavior that you seek. Show them how it's done because you become their measuring stick. The bible is clear as to us becoming models of behavior. Paul says to Timothy, "Don't let anyone look down on you because you are young, but set an example for the believers in speech, in life, in love, in faith and in purity". Paul was telling young Timothy that it his responsibility to model the life, love, and faith that he vehemently desired from the Christians in that day. Jesus gives us a model of how to war with the enemy. In Luke 4:4, "As it is written, Man shall not live on bread alone". This model is simply indicative of the fact that we must use the Word of God as our weapon on the enemy. What a model! This is the story of the Christian life. We should all strive to be conformed to the image of the Son. A good trainer always exemplifies desired behavior.

They Will Monitor You

Jesus is our ultimate model of leadership. In Matthew 14, Jesus comes to his disciples walking on water and they "saw" him approaching. This is indication that there was observation and monitoring. I'm writing this book going into my seventh year of ministry. After seven years, I've learned a great deal about people. My ministry profile is unique in the sense that we have young people, middle age, and a few elders as well. Across the generations one thing has been consistent, they all monitor me. By monitoring, I mean that they are all watching me to see how I respond to certain things, how I operate in ministry, how I live, how I treat my wife and family, how I spend money, how I treat everyone, how I act, etc. I believe it was such a shock to me at first because I didn't expect it. If you are reading this book and you are becoming offended, mad, or frustrated because certain individuals in your ministry are watching your every move, don't be. Just know that they will monitor you and that is only healthy because it keeps you disciplined and focused. The Apostle Paul already confirms that we have lives that are "epistles read of men" (2 Corinthians 3:2). Every move we make we should do so as if someone is watching and the first person we should be aware that is watching is God. It is that kind of accountability that keeps our reputations spotless and our names clear of integral scrutiny. I have become more selective now in where I go, what I do, and how I converse, mainly because there are individuals that are watching me and monitoring my every action. Your leadership team would especially love to monitor you and keep up with your travel. They love knowing where you are so that at any given time they can reach you. What I have discovered is that many of them will want to know where you are so that if you were in any danger they will know how to get there to provide protection for you in an expedient fashion. Very few of them will begin to learn your weakness and strengths. By them monitoring you, it will help them to see areas of growth from you but may also begin to show them a more intimate side of you that they have never seen. Remember, when you are dealing with anyone who partners with your ministry are sure to deal with them as if everyone is watching. My pastor, Pastor Freddie B. Carpenter of Bethel Missionary Baptist Church in Lascassas, Tennessee, once told me "Son, remember now, when you talk to one assume that you are talking to all of them". In other words, act, talk, and walk as if everyone can hear or see you. Be very careful what you say and when you say it. As leaders, it is as if we are held to a higher, more difficult standard than everyone else. We can't have bad days! We can't make a slip of the tongue. We can't afford to be sick and take time off. Obviously we can, but it begins to feel like this because everyone that is in the ministry or organization you lead will be monitoring you! Isn't it strange that these hawk-eye standards will be used and enforced with you but often times you can't use the same standard with them? However, this is what we asked for! Assume the role and accept it. They are going to monitor us and they should. In my opinion, it keeps us aligned with the will of God. Just recently we celebrated an anniversary in our ministry. I made what seemed to be a very self-centered and egotistical statement to some of my core group of leaders. It wasn't a statement directed at anyone or any group of people but that is the way some of them took it. The statement was made out of frustration which addressed a piercing claim thrown at me. After analyzing the situation and the statement, I was convicted. It was not the time, place or setting to make such a statement. I apologized to all of those involved and told them why it was said. I was wrong for the statement and the timing was just bad. I also addressed the issue which prompted me to make the statement as well. This was very important because until that point I had not had to defend something I said. It was a learning experience for me and the biggest lesson is that people will take everything you as the leader say to heart. Because we are being watched so closely, we have to be a little bit more selective about what we say and how we say it. I remember vividly my wife Toya had just lost a family member and was pretty sad that week, even on Sunday. She wept almost the entire service. Well, people were consoling her thinking it to be some marital issue between the two of us. Many thought she was experiencing some ministry burnout and it was finally coming out. This was not at all the problem; but since we are being closely watched, people will speculate about your life and your ministry. That is just part of the territory. I'm being so personal in this chapter because I want you to understand that as you are building your team, they are watching your every move; even when you don't think they are watching you, that is when they are watching the most.

They Will Mimic You

In Matthew chapter 14, as previously mentioned, Jesus comes walking on the water but then based on what the disciples saw in him, Peter desired to operate with the same power. He wanted to mimic his master! This is how people are! Arguably, the best player to ever play the game of basketball was Michael Jordan. I remember as a child seeing Jordan hit buzzer beaters, jump shots, and lead the team in such a passionate and first class manner. His actions made kids from all ages wanted to "Be like Mike". Gatorade promoted several commercials which became the banner for Jordan's career. Everyone wanted to be like him. The tagline read like this:

> "Sometimes I dream that he is me
> You've got to see that's how I dream to be
> I dream I move, I dream I groove
> Like Mike
> If I could Be Like Mike
> Again I try
> Just need to fly
> For just one day if I could
> Be that way
> I dream I move
> I dream I groove
> Like Mike
> If I could Be Like Mike". (Rovell)

The old saying is true: "Imitation is the highest form of flattery". What an honor for you to do something so worthy that people would not only want to do what you do, but also want to do it like you do it. All over the nation, aspiring basketball players were driving to the lane with their tongues out, hanging in the air trying to hit the shot. They were counting down the last second shot in the back yard and wearing baggy shorts with the wristband about the elbow trying to be like Mike. In your ministry, you are the closest model they have to leadership in ministry. Here is a bit of a newsflash, they will desire to be like you. Not only will they want to be in ministry but they will want to know how you study, how you plan, how you prepare, how you dress, how you conduct yourself, after all they will want to mimic you. This section is so personal for me because as I talked to Pastor Burnout, I remember him saying that over the years, ministers tried to preach like him and he told them, "You can't wear my armor David, get your own!" Or he would tell them that they could not handle his anointing and they should seek God for their own. Pastor Burnout shared how he would often correct them if they tried to use a quote from him. If the ministers asked to stand in on his behalf in his absence and they carried on as if he would, it would offend him. He would think they were trying to be him and take his place. When he shared this with me, I cringed because this kind of ideology is so crushing. It kills the dreams and hopes of young ministers and leaders. Most of the time, if we train ministers at all, we do so out of our own practice and regiment. Pastor Burnout wouldn't train ministers how God had put it on his heart to study, plan, and prepare. I sought God on what I could say to him after that because I felt that was so selfish of him. I remember it like it was yesterday; I sat up in my chair and asked him, "Were you insecure or afraid of their anointing?" He said, "Yes I was!" Personally, I believe that it is of high honor when my ministers quote me or use some teaching that I have used. I am proud when they conduct a meeting the way I would. This says to me that they see something in my ministry that they want to mimic. I wouldn't want it any other way. I should be the example and model for everyone who falls under my tutelage. They shouldn't have to look outside of you for a model. If they should be like anyone they should be like you because you are their leader. My father used to say, "A child shouldn't look outside of the home to find a role model." In a like manner, those who partner with you in ministry shouldn't have to look outside the spiritual house for a role model. After all, would you want it any other way? Think about it! What if you had five different leaders and they all sought to do things like someone else outside of the ministry. It would be total chaos. Even Paul the Apostle encourages leaders and believers alike to be like him and encouraged them to imitate his walk and life:

> I beseech you therefore, be ye imitators of me. **(1 Corinthians 4:16)**
>
> Be ye imitators of me, even as I also am of Christ. **(1 Corinthians 11:1)**
> Brethren, be ye imitators together of me, and mark them that so walk even as ye have us for an ensample. **(Philippians 3:17)**
>
> And ye became imitators of us, and of the Lord, having received the word in much affliction, with joy of the Holy Spirit. **(1 Thessalonians 1:6)**
>
> For ye, brethren, became imitators of the churches of God, which are in Judaea in Christ Jesus: for ye also suffered the same things of your own countrymen, even as they did of the Jews. **(1 Thessalonians 2:14)**
>
> That ye be not sluggish, but imitators of them who through faith and patience inherit the promises. **(Hebrews 6:12)**

It is interesting that Paul requested them to imitate him but Pastor Burnout would often chasten them for trying to imitate. Wow! The answer is simple! There is a natural inquisition to be like the leader. They will automatically like the way you teach, preach, etc. It is more than likely why they chose to join your ministry. How you develop them will determine how long they stay. Be careful who you push away or who you try to keep from imitating your style. Even if they have their own giftedness, let them use your style and presentation as a base. At Zion, I tell the ministers when they first come; ministry can be compared to a soldier learning to use their weapon for the first time. My job is to act as the Instructor that shows you at least how to use the weapon. It doesn't mean they don't sincerely have the gift it just means they have not learned how to use it. If they are unskilled with their weapon, it is because no one has properly showed them how to use it. They are going to mimic someone, so why not let that someone be you.

They Will Misread You

Going back to Matthew 14, the story progresses and as Jesus approaches the disciples walking on water, they were not sure if it was him or not. One of the roadblocks in any organization will be the ambiguities that exist between the leader and the team. If they are uncertain about the leader's expectation, it will create a problem. This issue could lead to major breakdowns in the flow and continuity of the whole project. I can truly say this is still a challenge for me. Sometimes, the team will take me the wrong way. They will misread my actions, thoughts, and intentions. God convicted me on this issue because I thought that if they didn't understand me, it was their fault. By revelation, I understood that they will only know of me what I allow them to know. If we as leaders are not careful we will blame others for the uncertainty in the ministry. I have discovered that these ambiguities lead to confusion. Progression is usually not born out of confusion. Leadership guru Samuel R. Chand adds to this way of thinking in his book entitled *Cracking Your Church's Culture Code*, he says:

> "People don't thrive in confusion. When a leader charts a clear course, the staff may ask a lot of questions before they get on board, and some may drag their feet for a long time before they embrace the skipper's map, but understanding is an essential element of a healthy work environment. Some leaders don't invite questions when they make their pronouncement of the future. Maybe they're not too sure about it themselves... A clear grasp

of the direction of the organization, though, is essential for the entire to be alignment and teamwork in each area of ministry. Without it, people wander, complain, doubt their leaders, chart their own course, or leave to find better leaders. Unpredictable leaders produce tentative followers!" (Chand)

People often misread us as leaders because we have not spent more time communicating to them our vision, expectations, and hearts. We must spend more time telling them what we want as opposed to telling them what we don't want. I believe that it is taking a proactive approach. I remember Pastor Burnout expressing to me his frustrations when Associate Ministers in his ministry would do things contrary to what he expected. He would become extremely furious. When I asked why, he said "they should know better". I would labor to say that this is a very popular paradigm, especially with pastor that have a low level of trust. In reality, Pastor Burnout mentioned that he spent no time telling them what he expected them to do but would wait until they messed up to correct them. This style of leadership will frustrate the team. Eventually, they will desire to move on or leave the ministry. When that happens, like Pastor Burnout, they will be left bitter blaming everyone else. I suggest that in order to get them to correctly read you, there needs to be implementation of two major techniques. They are very simple and practical. We must communicate and collaborate.

I would like to say that effective communication can be related to an author who wrote a book waiting to be published. For the book to make the connection to its readers, the author has to effectively communicate the purpose or intent of the book and carry the reader's attention for the duration of the of the writing. This is accomplished only if the author possesses the skill to structure the book to allow for easy reading. More than likely, the individuals that can follow along will eventually begin to understand. Some readers will continue long enough that the desire to understand remains. With that in mind, the author must guide every reader with the etching of their pen and capture their intellect in order to keep them interested. In the same way, we must effectively communicate with those who are partnering with our ministry. We must continue to find ways to communicate with them. Most of the time, it involves adapting to the current technological advancements. Whether its conference calls, video chats, mass emails, mass text messages, web applications, mobile apps, or simple face to face meetings, we must find creative ways to communicate. If there is a breakdown in the communication, your participants will misread you and often take what you say and do the wrong way. In order to avoid that kind of breakdown, it is imperative that you spend a little time with them. Tell them how you want things done and express the matters of your heart. Take this time to share with them their limitations and freedoms within the organization. This will help them to function with a little more ease because they understand whether they are doing much or little, they are doing what pleases you. It will be worth it to create collaborative projects with your team in order to promote the idea of unity. There are some things that you can't do on your own. Some things that you may not need to originate; open the opportunity to allow more team members to involve themselves in some of the decision making or planning of the organization. This allows them passage to experience the ministry from your shoes. It gives you opportunity to communicate to them how you want things done. Apply this process and instruct them in your ways of operation. By default, it will reduce their confusion and eliminate ambiguity in most cases. To ensure successful and useful communication, allow your communication to be governed by these three standards that are suggested in John Maxwell's *17 Indisputable Laws of Leadership*:

>**Be Consistent.** Nothing frustrates team members more than leaders who can't make up their minds.
>
>**Be Clear.** Your team cannot execute if they don't know what you want. Don't try to dazzle anyone with your intelligence; impress him or her with your simple straightforwardness.
>
>**Be Courteous.** Everyone deserves to be shown respect, no matter what his or her position or what kind of history you might have with them. If you are courteous to

your people, you set a tone for the entire organization. (Maxwell, The 17 Indisputable Laws of Teamwork)

As a leader, I must admit, there is nothing more frustrating than for the team to do something that you have not suggested or desired. I had to learn that if this takes place often then, there must be a breakdown in my communication in some way. Maybe something in my communication was not clear; Maybe, I had to reassess my method of communication to allow for more simplicity. Effective communication will in most cases keep people from misreading you. In my organization, we have at least 6 forms of communication. This is to attempt to keep an open connection with the people involved. If they still misread you, then you must investigate problems at the other end of the communication. Maybe there is a barrier between them receiving the communication.

Motivating: Encourage them To Launch

I've already mentioned how I believe that Jesus Christ is our ultimate leadership model. Earlier, we used a passage in Matthew 14: 25-31. After Jesus came closer to the disciples, walking on water, Peter wanted to mimic the master and asked if he could walk on water, too. Jesus shifts from being a modeler in his leadership to being a motivator. He sums it up in one word, "Come!" It is not strange that many people on your team would love for you to motivate them. Some of them will need you to call them out of the boat of complacency to into the risky sea of opportunity. As a leader, not only should you model the behavior you seek, but you should also motivate them to launch out. Jesus was a developer. He loved "making" disciples. I believe that every effective leader should also be a developer. To see a shy, timid, team member progress to a bold, powerful, impactful leader is rewarding to me. It is why I do it! Ken Blanchard calls it "performance coaching". In his book, *Lead like Jesus*, he explains the role of the motivator or performance coach:

There are three parts to becoming a performance coach: performance planning is all about providing direction and setting goals, day-to-day coaching, and performance evaluation. Performance planning is providing direction and setting goals. Day-to-day coaching involves helping people win-accomplishing goals by observing their performance, praising progress, and redirecting efforts that are off base. The final part of performance coaching: performance evaluation. It requires sitting down with people and evaluating their performance over time. (Hodges)

Motivating is a gradual and persistent thing. It will not suffice to just do it every once and a while. We must strategically and consistently plan for the motivating of our team members and dedicate time to coach them along the way. Like Peter, they need to know that they too can launch out and challenge the impossible. Sometimes, team members will need confirmation from you in order to unlock the potential that is inside them. We must remember that as senior leaders, we are charged with the responsibility of development and discipleship those who are with us. Walter A. Henrichsen suggests,

"A disciple must learn to believe in himself. I am crucified with Christ, nevertheless I live; yet not I, but Christ lives in me; and the life which I now live in the flesh I live by faith of the Son of God, who loved me and gave himself for me" (Galatians 2:20). In this verse, we see two 'I's'- the crucified "I" and the resurrected "I" (Henrichsen).

In training, we work hard at crucifying the old "I" but spend little time in helping a disciple resurrect the new "I" in Christ. We must have no confidence in flesh, but at the same time, we must believe that we can "do all things through Christ". Part of the development of each leader is to gain confidence in them to such a degree that every door that is opened for them, they are prepared to walk through it. Many of the lay leaders will become burned out if the senior leaders are not motivators. This leads to mass burnout. Let's take time to discover why we need to motivate.

They Will Be Fearful

Any leader that anticipates longevity in the ministry must overcome a mountain of fears. Fears cause all of us to stay complacent and often times, hinders our potential and progress. One of the biggest lessons those leaders must learn is how to cope with or overcome fears. In our text, Matthew 14:30, something about Peter is central to the heart of motivators in leadership. It says, "But when he saw the wind boisterous, he was afraid". The "he" is Peter and his problem was his fear. Peter saw that the wind was boisterous and he became fearful! This is why many leaders need to be motivated. They cannot handle all that comes with the assignment initially. Peter was excited to jump out of the boat and mimic the master but he didn't know that he would soon experience boisterous winds. What is inarguably clear is that as soon as we shift our focus from completing the task to what is going on around us, we become afraid. How many times have you seen this? It happens all over the world. Leaders will start fresh ministries or they will start out with new projects with such excitement. However, as soon as a few winds blow or a few people frustrate them, they become fearful. As the senior leader, you will have to become the motivator through unwanted fears. There are three things about fear that you can share with your team that will motivate them through the boisterous winds.

Fear is Allowed

Those of us who have been afraid or walked in fear have done so because we have allowed fear to come into our lives and take residence in our minds. The reality is we don't have to be afraid. 2 Timothy 1:7 reminds us, "God has not given us a spirit of fear, but of power, love and of a sound mind". This means if it is not God's will for us to walk in fear, why do we continue to do so? Motivate your leaders to not allow fear to control their minds, hearts, nor actions. People who are controlled by fear accomplish very little because they are afraid of the future. With great achievements comes the reality of great risks. Fearful people take very little risks. They play it safe. They never operate on faith! If you have a team full of timid, fearful, and hesitant leaders on your team, it will be difficult for your organization to expand. As the senior leader, you can help them overcome their fears by motivating them and encouraging them not to be afraid of the boisterous but necessary winds of life.

Fear is Avoidable

To a certain degree, fears can be avoided. The only way we can avoid fears is to be motivated behind a purpose and confident in its results. Sometimes the anxiety of seeing something through can overwhelm us. It doesn't necessarily mean that you are scared, but just extra cautious about the success of something. Fear can be avoided by having proper motivation from a leader and trust that transcends trials. Most people that partner with a church or religious institution will do so because of their commitment to God and not the leader per se. In this instance, the motivation to do a thing comes from within the person. Their dedication to the Savior speaks louder than their dedication to the supervisor. However, the leader must still take that motivational factor and begin to aim it and cultivate it. To avoid future fear, one must be emphatically empowered. Notice what Curtis Wallace writes:

> "The great thing about working with a church staff is that, on a certain level, motivation is easy. The people, for the most part, have joined the staff because they want to be a part of the broader meaning and significance that working in a religious organization can provide. Unlike a career in a law firm or a large corporation, where satisfaction comes from the quality of the work and making money, there is a larger purpose at work here. Great church staffers are responding to a higher calling. The result is that your staff should largely be "pre-motivated" (Wallace).

Now you just need to harness that motivation and point it in the right direction.

They Will Be Faithless

As we progress through Matthew chapter 14, verse 31 shows us something very profound about Peter. Jesus challenges Peter in the area of his faith. He asked him, "O ye of little faith, why did you doubt?" It seems to me that Peter exemplified a great deal of faith and especially more faith that the other disciples demonstrated. Why does the master challenge his faith? It took faith for Peter to acknowledge the Lord walking on the water. It took even greater faith for Peter to believe that he, too, could do the impossible and walk on the water. Interestingly, Jesus challenges his faith because Peter allowed the things happening around him to distract him and somewhere in the distraction his faith waivered. The Bible tells us "set your mind to be right-minded, even as God has dealt to every man the measure of faith". (Holy Bible, Word Search Corp.) The mere fact that every man has a measure of faith should let you know that not everyone in your organization or on your team will believe in the vision, values, or variables like you do. Sometimes, just like Peter, they are distracted by what could go wrong, what could be potentially harmful, or what deal could slip through! They have been infected with the faithless! Many people will be ineffective because they have lost faith. Yet, they are on your team. When Jesus's disciples could not cast out a demon, He said they were part of a faithless and perverse generation. The interesting thing is that Jesus did not get rid of them nor did He tell them that they needed to find some training or schooling either. Time and time again, with patience, Jesus continued to "make" them into fishers of men. The disciples were made, not born. Some leaders have strong faith in one area and weak faith in others. It is your responsibility as the senior leader to cultivate every gift and piece of potential in all of those that partner with your ministry. Faith can sometimes be triggered. It can be strengthened with strong motivation. In Philippians 1, Paul speaks in regard to others "waxing more bold to speak" because of his chains. It helps to fortify an individual's faith if you take time to motivate them in times of hardship or despair. Over my years of pastoring, I really found out that people respect and regard the words of their leader. Sometimes your words are what people use to make it through the week. When I began to understand that even on a more personal level, many of the people in my ministry didn't have fathers, mothers, or positive parental figures. Just as we begin to seek out confirmation from those people of influence early in life, that's when we commit to a leader. We look for "well done" or "you can do it". It heightens our level of belief at all levels. Not everyone in your ministry or organization will have super-natural or jaw dropping faith. Some will be as shallow in their faith as they are in their theology. But we must remember all they need is a mustard seed for God to work a miracle. As the leader, since you didn't write the standard of how much faith is required, you must keep in mind that you can't run away from individuals with weak or small amounts of it. Never get discouraged with people who have little faith. Keep teaching, preaching, and ministering the Word of God, because the more they hear it, the more their faith is developed. It is not the fact that people become faithless that I'm concerned about. It is the mere fact that when they are faithless, we become discouraged, disappointed, or depressed. Free yourself from that! To help you avoid feeling that way, whether it is about them or because of them, try Faith Assessments, Faith Assignments, and Faith Attitudes.

Faith Assessments

Faith is strengthened best when it is tested. I spent six years as a Firefighter in the city of Murfreesboro. I learned a huge lesson on testing while I served there. I remember fire engineers would test the hoses so they would be good for actual use. Every year, the fire hoses would have to be tested by state requirements. What I found interesting was that each hose had to test out at certain levels in order to be deemed worthy to be placed on the fire apparatus. In order to do the test, the hose the engineer would hook the hose to the pump and turn the pressure up to an elevated level to see if the hose could withstand the pressure. If the hose endured without bursting or leaking at a coupling, then it would pass the test and be ready for use. Like the hose, we must pass the test. Sometimes in order to test us, we have to be put under extreme pressure. If we can endure the pressure, we will be qualified for future usage. I love the way James puts it in James 1:2-3, "My brethren, count it all joy when ye fall into divers temptations; Knowing this, that the trying of your faith worketh patience." (Holy Bible, Word Search Corp.) In order to assess the faith of those in your ministry, we must watch how they handle pressure. Many leaders cannot handle the pressures that come with ministry or life. This will subtract from their giftedness and sometimes hinder their effectiveness. They may be graced to minister through song, but when faced with the task of managing people's personalities and attitudes, it can frustrate them. Often times, it can strip them of their confidence. I'm hardly ever too impressed with gifted and talented people until I've seen them do it under pressure. I believe that this is the truest assessment of faith. Put them in situations that will require strong faith and consistent expectation. I would often gain a little more respect from individuals whose faith would remain intact through personal stress and strain. I have had to preach through some very trying times in my life that tested my faith. Some of my best sermons have been preached when I was having marital issues, lost a loved one, and yes, even when I didn't understand what God was doing in my life. These were defining moments in my faith. It was almost as if my faith was strengthened in such weak moments. I would challenge any senior leader to assess their faith through something. Watch how they handle defeat, discouragement, or detriment. These will help you discover whether they are faithless or faithful.

Faith Assignments

I'll never forget my early ministry. I was 19 years old when I first started ministering and 20 years old when I began preaching. I remember the first time I had ever gone out to preach away from my home church. It was at a church that was very well known in the area and the pastor was out of town for the weekend. I remember the details vividly because my pastor had called me and told me to go and fill in, but I had no knowledge of that pastor, his church, their structure, flow, or ministry style. The fact that it was communion Sunday didn't help any either. I guess I was just thrown in the fire! This was a very life changing experience because it made me grow up real quick. I had to cram in some last minute research, call a few pastor friends, and boy, did I have to pray. It unlocked a new level of faith in me. This was a "faith assignment". Faith assignments will mature your leaders. It will cause them to personally dig deep and then it will cause them to have a dependence on God that no one can give them but the Lord. Jesus would always give the disciples faith assignments. Thomas had issues with doubt, so Jesus gave him an assignment. He told him to "touch the nail prints in his hands". Even Peter, who had already shown a history of shaky faith and even denied Christ, still received instruction from the Lord to "feed His sheep". Surely, we can't forget Abraham, whom God told to "go to a land I will show you". This came with a price because Abraham would have to leave some things behind that were of comfort. In order to exercise our faith, we have to have an assignment. I will tell you that if your leaders don't have assignments, they will become like most of the tools in your garage. They will get rusty because they are not getting used. Give them something to do! No matter how small the task, if they are kept busy, it lessens the risk of them focusing on distractions. Idleness will kill faith quicker than anything.

They Will Sometimes Fail

As we move through this story of Matthew 14 we come to verse 30. It tells us that Peter began to sink into the water after he caught a glimpse of the surrounding conditions. It reminds us that sometimes as leaders, we fall and those who partner with the ministry will fall if they continue to serve in a leadership capacity. I've seen pastors become discouraged and disconnected to leaders who fall. This will eventually lead to burnout. Sometimes you put so much stock in people and you never factor in how they may make mistakes or miss the mark. I think what we must do as leaders is become aware of the fact that people will fail. If we don't anticipate or expect people to fail, we become easily frustrated and agitated with them. This will cause unwanted tension, because people will eventually start to depart from any leader that doesn't give room for mistakes. This will cancel the principle of participation and as I mentioned before, we can become burned out. If we possibly change our perception of failure, we wouldn't get so bent out of shape when people do it. The difference between greatness and mediocrity is often how an individual views a mistake (Maxwell, Failing Forward). Every leader at some point has failed with their lifestyle choices, and some kind of ministry launch.

Leadership Failures

Everyone who has skill, talent, or gifts are blessed beyond measure and favored of God. However, this doesn't mean that they are qualified to lead and be successful at it. I have met people who have more skill than anyone in the room but their downfall was they lacked the proper leadership skills. Some people pass the test of talent, but fail miserably in leading. As the senior leader, we must be prepared and patient enough to develop leaders out of both talented and both untalented. Just imagine how much more effective an individual could be if they were to use their skill and begin to lead others as well. The truest form of leadership begins when we are noted as being people of influence. Jesus was a prolific preacher and a tactical teacher. However, I believe his most notable quality was his ability to lead. He possessed a sphere of influence that has never been matched. The way Jesus was able to take ordinary men and women and convince them to leave their jobs to follow him was an exceptional display of leadership. At some point, leaders should be able to glance back and experience defining moments in their leadership. Not everyone will possess this kind of leadership quality. Some individuals are better followers than they are leaders. As a senior leader, you must be aware of that and not beat them up for falling short of the leadership standard. Be dedicated to developing and helping them grow in this aspect.

Lifestyle Failures

Let me begin with the Word of God on this part of the book. The Bible says in Romans 3:23 that "All have sinned and fallen short of the glory of God" (Holy Bible, Word Search Corp.). This means that sooner or later, there will be some character flaw in some of your leaders. Sin will leave its crimson stain. Please understand that people will have enough blame and ridicule to lay on a fallen leader without you as the senior leader adding to the finger pointing. The Bible clearly states in Galatians 6:1, "Brethren, if a man be overtaken in a fault, ye which are spiritual, restore such a one in the spirit of meekness; considering thyself, lest thou also be tempted" (Holy Bible, Word Search Corp.). We should be there to restore, redirect, and renew them. I've seen ministries crumble, churches split, and marriages torn apart because a leader fell. I'm not saying that we should compromise either. There should be a standard of righteousness to uphold. We should demand that of our leaders and there should be consequence if the standards aren't met. I think we should consider the fact that we all have two laws working in us and sometimes that other law wins. As the senior leader, it is easy to get discouraged when you feel surrounded by people who just don't get it. Their lifestyle doesn't match their anointing. Be encouraged in the simple fact that God knew he could trust you to develop that person. Be the standard, live the standard, value the standards, and require it. In the event that one of your leaders have lifestyle failures, love them through the fall, restore them and see how you will have a deeper level of commitment from them.

Launching Failures
When you think about launching failures, you often think about rockets or space shuttles that don't take off properly. Sometimes we launch ministry ideas that can't get off the ground. Somewhere they have started out of the blocks but then came tumbling down. When leaders have launch failures, it could be years before they try it again. As the senior leader, one way to always have participation is to keep those who partner with your ministry motivated to progress their own ministry along with the vision of organization. This keeps a consistent progression that can be beneficial to the church as well as to the individual. For every ministry launch or idea we have, there will probably be an equal amount of failures. You might plant a church two times before you get it right. There may be three non-profits before the fourth one kicks off. The point is, we can't get discouraged when we try and it doesn't succeed. My dear friend Pastor Burnout would often get upset with his associate ministers who tried something and it didn't work out. He said he would look at them and say things like, "Just do what I tell you to do"! I had to help Pastor Burnout change his perception

on failure so that he could lead them differently. Listen to John C. Maxwell:

> "There's an old saying in Texas: 'It doesn't matter how much milk you spill as long as you don't lose your cow'. In other words, mistakes are not irreversible. Keep everything in perspective. The problems come when you see only the spilled milk and not the bigger picture. People who correctly see failure take it in stride. Mistakes don't make them want to give up. Success doesn't make them think that they are set up (Maxwell, Failing Forward).

Many, if not most, of the leaders in your organization will fail at some initiative. Our responsibility should be to encourage them to launch again. Suggest new methods but with the same enthusiam and excitement. Remember, they are there to support you, follow you, and uplift you. It would not hurt to show them that you can do the same for them. This solidifies a healthy relationship and keeps them bought in for the long haul.

Mentoring: Taking a Passive Role

As we walk through Matthew chapter 14, the narrative continues to give us fresh insight to Jesus's leadership qualities. I noticed that when Jesus came to them walking on the water, He motivated Peter to participate. He did not go and hold Peter's hand nor approach the boat; He simply challenged Peter to come to him. He first appeared as a Model because He showed them how to walk on water. He then became a motivator when He told Peter to come to him. I will point out that He has taken the role of a mentor because He allowed Peter room to come to Him without being so involved that it handicapped Peter. I believe these leadership roles happen progressively. Sometimes leaders need you to be all three and other times you only need to be one. The goal, however, is to model, motivate, and become a mentor. When mentoring people, you must always take a passive role. Humility has to undergird your thinking when mentoring. In order to be passive, you must be humble enough not to rush in and immediately take control of someone's ministry or life. We have a tendency to do that if we are not careful. If you have already gone to the extreme of modeling and motivating, then you have gotten the bulk of your work done. You must genuinely care and love a person to successfully serve them and mentor them. You will have a natural feeling of responsibility to individuals you mentor. Henry Blackaby says this,

> "Leaders who are unable to love their people and who are unwilling to consider their needs are insecure in their own identity. Why was Jesus able to humble Himself and wash His disciples' filthy feet? The scripture says "Jesus, knowing that the Father had given all things into His hands, and that He had come forth from God, and was going back to God....Jesus knew where had come from and where He was going. He was not insecure about His identity. His self-worth was not on the line. He was dead center in his Father's will and He knew it. That made all the difference" (Blackaby).

We should mentor people from a place of solidarity. I know who I am. I know whose I am. I have enough sense to know that learning must be experiential for the person being mentored. This leads me to share with you a few things about mentoring. It means we should lead from a distance, listen for a demand, and limit our duties.

Lead from a Distance
It took me a while but I finally figured out that you don't have to call, email, or talk to people every day for them to learn from you. People will watch the senior leader. They learn from your messages, mannerisms, and methods. People will literally study the leader in order to glean from them a reference for leadership. People were being touched by my leadership that I didn't even know. They watched me! Sometimes you can have such an influence on people you don't know because you figured out how to lead from a distance. I believe once you have provided a model then you have to allow people to experience some things

on their own. Clearly, people's life experiences can greatly affect the kind of leaders they become. Something as basic as birth order can have a profound impact on one's development as a leader. Typically, oldest children are more likely to lead because they are generally given more responsibility by their parents. They often have a greater sense of affiliation with their parents than their younger siblings. "Their superiority in size, strength, and knowledge compared to their younger siblings gives them confidence and enables them to begin exercising leadership in their homes at an early age" (Blackaby). The point is, they have been given the opportunity to experience life for themselves. Sooner or later, you have to take the training wheels off and tell the leaders go ahead, "I'll be over here". If you don't learn to mentor, you will attempt to model before people and motivate people for long periods of time. This will drain your energy and eventually cause you to burn out! Take a season to just watch them go, so to speak. I remember when my dad taught me how to ride a bike. The very first thing he did was give me all the information on the bike. He taught me what kind of bike, how many gears it had, etc. Then he got on it and modeled riding it. Then he steadied me on the bike and said "O.K., now it's your turn. You can do it". After that, he began to mentor me. He stood off to the side and watched as I rode the bike. Every once and a while, he issued verbal instructions to me for my bike ride. Mentoring is all about leading from a distance. Let me relieve you of all the stress of your overactive leadership style today. Back off a little! That is, of course, if you have already provided the first two leadership methods.

Listen for a Demand

When Peter came walking on the water and began to sink, Jesus never reached out to catch Peter until he called out for Jesus to help him. Sometimes the hardest thing to do is to refrain from stepping in and try to save people. Naturally, we want to fix the problem and run in giving instruction immediately. Doing this, you will get burned out quicker than you think. When mentoring people, you always wait for a demand. Much too often, we try and help people in areas that they have not asked us to help them in. This will confuse them and can sometimes create unwanted problems and pressures in your relationships with them. There is nothing worse than receiving criticism and advice that you didn't ask for. I've seen that crush confidence quicker than anything. I remember mentoring a minister at our church who had to go and preach at another ministry. My propensity to instruct had taken over and I just wanted to help. Immediately, I began sharing how I would do it and say it. The preacher ended up preaching his own sermon, with his own methods. I thought to myself, "Why didn't they use what I had shown him? I gave him all this stuff". The reality is that even though I gave him all of this material, I had to realize that he didn't ask for it. I learned a valuable lesson that day. As I mentor, I'm only going to move when people ask.

Limit Your Duties
I think that it will be important for us all to remember that we shouldn't try and do too much as relates to leadership. Mentors have figured out a way to limit their duties in their followers' lives. You can't get so involved that you become overwhelmed with every detail of their lives. When Peter started sinking, Jesus only caught him and helped him up. He didn't do anything more. Sometimes all our leaders need is a hand to get up. Don't try doing it for them. Don't give them more instruction or show them how to do everything, etc. Sometimes it is way too much. Mentor them instead. Simply help them up and send them back on their way. Sometimes, we stunt the growth of the individuals on our team by doing everything for them. Not only do we stunt their growth, but we miss out on growth opportunities ourselves by constantly do things for the team. In his book, *Leadership Gap*, Curtis Wallace asserts, "a leader who insists on doing everything will be limited-you can only do so much" (Wallace). If Pastor Burnout was to speak on this issue, he would say, "Well, I tried to let them do it but they just didn't do it right! So I'll do it myself!" Free yourself from burnout today. Don't try and be a dictator or control freak, mentor your people. You don't want the bondage of that responsibility.

"In order for any organization to survive and thrive, there has to be a visionary at the top. When you have a visionary at the top and the visionary has time to behave like a visionary, the organization will have that all-important rudder to guide its direction. Look at what I've just said. The leader has to have time to be a visionary and he or she has to behave like a visionary. In all organizations, but in religious organizations specifically, this is hugely important. The leader of the organization by definition must be in concert with God's will and desire for the organization. That means the leader must be free to spend the time it takes to behave like a visionary. This means the time to study, pray, and think about where the organization is headed, what the organization is doing, and how it is managing its resources. The leader can't accomplish this objective if he or she is spending all of his or her time trying to tend to the myriad of details of running growing organizations. It means that you can't be a visionary if you have other people to run the organization but you don't let them do their jobs" (Wallace).

Like Pastor Burnout, few leaders never let go of insecurities and fear and began to mentor their leaders. It doesn't involve you all the time. The situations may request you but it must be understood that it doesn't require you. Don't do too much.

3T Discussion
1. What kind of training method are you applying? Are you a mentor, model, or motivator?

3T Discovery
Try applying each leadership training method this week. Use all three!

CHAPTER 3

Trust Them

In the previous chapter we finished by telling you to mentor leaders with more a passive role without doing everything for them. There is only one crucial reason why we will not lead people from a distance and that is we don't trust them. My question is why? If you taught them, and trained them, why wouldn't you trust them? There can be several reasons why we don't trust people. First, we don't trust because of their past. Maybe they have had a history of betrayal or selfishness. Maybe that person has wronged us in the past and we carry that hurt or bad experience with us into future projects. Whatever the reason, if the person is still a part of the organization, then we must understand that we have an obligation as a leader to develop them. So, lets reason for a moment. Even if you don't trust the person you could possibly trust the investment you made in them. After all, they have already gone through the first two T's of ministry, haven't they? You have made an investment in their life, trust that. Trust that God is working in them. I know that some leaders will have us question whether God is even in them. The reality is that we can only trust that if they call on the name of the Lord, they are saved. If they have professed to serve God in leadership under your care, then you have to trust what God has done through your time of teaching and training them. Secondly, we don't trust because of personalities. Some of your leaders have unique personalities. Some people are quiet; some are very loquacious and seems as if they will never stop talking. Some are jokesters, some are intense and serious. These various types of personalities lead us to limit our trust for people. Thirdly, we don't trust because of empty promises. One way to lose my trust is to tell me you will do something and then don't do it. You will get this all the time from people. Leaders who don't show up to bible study, church, leadership meetings, or they don't fulfill certain obligations are all examples of individuals who don't keep their obligatory word. This reoccurrence of empty promises will cause us to lose trust in them. As much as you hate to hear it, you have to trust something. If not them, then trust the time you have spent with them. If you can't trust the time you have spent with them, trust the fact that you will keep teaching and training until they earn your trust. If not that, trust God! At the end of the day, unless you want to have no partnerships, participation, or progression, you have to trust them! Trust is all about releasing them. You have to let go of your grip on things and loosen your clinch. When you release them, here are some very practical directives that you should release them to do. This will save you some stress in the long run. Release them to be Followers of Christ, Fruitful for Christ, Feeders for Christ, and Faithful to Christ.

Release Them: To Be Followers of Christ

When training my ministers, I have a favorite saying, "Be Christian First, and then a Preacher". I believe that often times we lose perspective on the priorities of the Christian life. This causes us to live any kind of way and then fall into various traps set by the enemy. Matthew 6:33 reminds us to "Seek ye first the kingdom of God and his righteousness and everything else will be added to us". Before we seek elevation or promotion in the ministry we should seek to please God first. David was an illustrious king but when he sinned against God he sought to get it right with God first. His cry in Psalm 51:4 when speaking to God was "Against thee and thee only have I sinned and done this evil". His title and position didn't matter. He wanted to be right with God. Then there is the powerful statement from Jesus himself as to the requirements for following him. He says in Matthew 16:24, "If anyone would come after me, let him deny himself and take up his cross and follow me." Look at this passage a little closer. Jesus gives two imperatives for following him. In order to be a follower of Christ, we must first conquer self. At the most basic level, self-discipline is the ability to do what is right even when you don't feel like doing it. Outstanding leaders and achievers throughout history understood this. Greek philosopher Plato asserted, "The first and best victory is to conquer self" (Maxwell, Talent is Never Enough Workbook). He said we must deny ourselves in order to follow him. Many leaders have not been prompted to live for Christ. We push agendas, promotions, projects, and conferences but very few are just promoting being followers of Christ. It requires us laying aside personal agendas and fleshly desires. When I deny self, I learn how to control fleshly desires. This will be very important in the future of the ministry. If you can learn to control your flesh which is constantly at war against God, you will be able to guard against future temptations and setbacks that may be a detriment to your character.

After we conquer self, we must then cling to suffering. Jesus goes on to tell us to take up our cross. I'm always bothered by the number of people who want the pleasures of the Christian life without enduring the pains of the Christian life. Many ministers and leaders want to jump straight to the success and omit the suffering. Jesus says that suffering defines His followers. Paul the apostle reminds us in Philippians 2 that Christ was obedient unto death. This means that He knew He was going to suffer and yet He persevered in spite of the pain and pressure. Maxwell comments on staying in when it's tough:

> "Perseverance is not an issue of talent. It is not an issue of time. It is about finishing. Talent provides hope for accomplishment, but perseverance guarantees it. Playwright Noel Coward commented, 'Thousands of people have talent. I might as well congratulate you for having eyes in your head.' The one and only thing that counts is whether or not you have staying power. (Maxwell, Talent is Never Enough Workbook)

We have enough money seeking, fame following preachers. Once you began to trust them, release them. Once you release them, release them first and foremost to follow Christ!

Release Them: To be Fruitful for Christ

When Jesus gives his disciples the great commission in Matthew 28:19-20, he does so with specific instruction. He says to them that they are to infiltrate the world, "go ye therefore into all the world", and through the illumination of God's word, "make disciples". We have been commissioned to bear the fruit of discipleship. Christ released them to be witnesses to other people. He released them to bring souls to Christ and as a result help them to become disciple makers. This is the fruit of the believer and should be the fruit of the leader. Bearing fruit is all about growth and development. In 2 Timothy 2:2 the Apostle Paul admonishes Timothy to "take the things that he has heard from him and entrust these to faithful men who will be able to teach others also". The question every leader should ask is, "where is the fruit of my labor?" Who has been saved? Who has been changed? Who has grown and matured? Who has been empowered as a result of my leadership and ministry? We should encourage leaders to be committed not only to making disciples but to maturing disciples. It is a process that never ends. Maturing disciples becomes the leader's fruit. There is no greater joy for me than to see a leader or minister that started in my ministry (that no one gave a chance) grow into a man or woman that God uses to have powerful influence. That is fruit that remains and comes at the hand and heart effective discipleship. I'm honored that God would the example of my life and the lessons in my leadership to plant seeds that will yield fruit in other lives. Colossians 1:10 says, "So as to walk in a manner worthy of the Lord, fully pleasing to him, bearing fruit in every good work and increasing in the knowledge of God". In other words, the more I increase my knowledge and experiences, the more I am able to share with others. My methods become their miracle to overcome obstacles in their lives.

In order to be a true disciple of Christ, we should bear fruit. Jesus says in John 15:8 "By this my Father is glorified, that you bear much fruit and so prove to be my disciples." Whenever God uses us as people of influence and we have released others to be fruitful as well, we must then be concerned with what kind of fruit we bear. The Bible says in Matthew 12:33, "Either make the tree good, and his fruit good; or else make the tree corrupt, and his fruit corrupt: for the tree is known by his fruit". In other words, we must be careful not to disciple people when we have character flaws gushing from our own lives. If we are hurt or wounded, then we will shape and mold hurt and wounded disciples. If we walk in offense, then we produce more leaders that walk in offense. We must guard ourselves and our ministries of this huge impropriety. What kind of leader are you developing? If you say, "I'm producing more leaders like me" then is that really a good thing or a bad one? You can't give up on leaders that don't look like you, act like you, talk like you, etc. The reality is you have been called to disciple them no matter where they are in their life because God has entrusted them to you. Getting mad and upset will only burn you out. Remember, if they have been in your ministry through the teaching and the training, the leader they are today is because you taught them that and even if your instruction was unintentional or purposeful, you still shaped them. Please encourage your leaders to be fruitful.

Release Them: To be Feeders

By now we should be a little bit more acquainted with the apostle Peter. His life was just one huge rollercoaster ride. Three times Peter denied Jesus and three times Jesus asked Peter if he loved him. In John 21:15-18, it records a dialogue between Peter and the Master. Three times, Peter said "yes, Lord I love you". Jesus says to him "feed my sheep". It gives Peter a shepherd- like quality. God still retains possession of the sheep because he said "My sheep", but he does not fall short of telling Peter that he will have to the responsibility of feeding them. No matter how common your relationship becomes with your leader you must remember God put them in your care for you to feed them. Use every opportunity you can to speak words of encouragement, equipping, and enlightening them through God's word. I'm not saying that you have to always be in "teach" mode. What I am saying is that it is necessary to lay the foundation that you are the senior leader with a primary task of feeding them. I've seen leaders allow people to come in with equal levels influence and eventually, lose their influence over the team because he or she stopped feeding them. Even something as simple as a card with encouraging scriptures, or a phone call with a moment of prayer with an uplifting word will go a long way in maintaining the proper relationship. Remember, it has all to do with how they see you. My prayer is that you don't get to the point that your leaders no longer see you as someone they can learn from. It becomes a detriment to both the vision of the ministry and the health of the leader. At that point, the sheep then tries to feed the shepherd. Keep feeding them at all cost. And even when they don't want to hear it, call to memory what Paul says to Timothy, "Preach the word; be instant in season, out of season; reprove, rebuke, exhort with all longsuffering and doctrine" (2 Timothy 4:2). Never slip on an opportunity to be a feeder. If you can maintain this kind of relationship with those who partner with your ministry, you will soon discover they will also strive to become feeders. Release them to be followers, fruitful, and feeders! Make sure we have given them the words of the Ecclesiastical writer, "The words of the wise are as goads, and as nails fastened by the masters of assemblies, which are given from one shepherd". (Ecclesiastes 12:11) This is what we are, "Masters of Assemblies". No matter how many gifted or talented people assemble in my ministry, God has placed me there as the "master of the assembly". Don't let insecurity creep in because God has blessed you with qualified leaders. Yes, they can preach, they can teach, they can sing, and they have influence, but and the end of the day, they have sat down at the table God has entrusted to you, so feed them! And when you have fed them, keep feeding until they are so full that they have to feed others and share the food. This will keep you off interstate "burnout". Please take this exit today, my beloved leader for God! If you are not releasing them to feed, they will become eaters. They will be hearers of the Word, but never doers! Trust them enough to let them go and feed someone, after all what they will use is what you taught them! So learn to trust! Hopefully, there is a leader in your ministry that comes to mind when you read this book. Please, take your grip off of them. You have trained them for years and you're trying to figure out why they have all of sudden stop agreeing with everything you say? Why are they no longer saying "Amen" to your messages? Why have they stopped becoming excited with your new visions and ideas? It is simple, beloved! Spiritually, they have become fat with your doctrines and didactics. Release them; it's time for them to feed others!

3T Discussion
    1.   What can you release them to do in your ministry?

3T Discovery
    If you had one person in your ministry that you could trust with your mantle, who would it be? If you could trust them, what would you release them to do? Will they have your training and tactics?

CHAPTER FOUR

I'm Not the Senior Leader

I almost ended this book without including this chapter but the Holy Spirit spoke to me and led me to speak to those of you who are reading this book and are not the senior leader. By "senior leader", I mean the one who is at the very top of the structure of the ministry or organization. My heart goes out to you because I have been there before. I was a lay leader who had very little influence or responsibility. Then, I became the middle person between the lay leaders and the senior leader. I have experience it from both sides. Even though the senior leader has self-contained concerns and struggles with managing people, I sympathize with you as well. I know it is very easy for you to get burned out. I would like to spend just a short period of time in this chapter ministering to you. Sometimes as leaders under the senior leader, we fight against ourselves. I want to share with you in this chapter some fundamentals or basics to approaching serving a leader who dedicates themselves to applying the 3T's of ministry that are talked about in this book. I agree with K. Edward Copeland when he says:

> "Creativity is hampered when the basics are not mastered. You cannot do calculus if you do to know how to multiply. You cannot write poetry if you do not understand sentence structure. You cannot become a chef if you do not know the difference between boiling and broiling. Regardless of the arena, you cannot reach your

full potential until you learn the basics. Once the fundamentals are grasped, however, there is no limit to what the Holy Spirit can create through human personality" (Copeland).

Be open to receive the basics of ministry so that you might develop into the minister and leader that God has called you to be. I'm excited about your future and I want you to experience everything that God has in store for you. I want to share with you three very practical directives that may help you become more receptive, respectful, and relational with a 3T senior leader. If the senior leader is attempting to teach you, train you, and trust you, then you must be teachable, trainable, and trustworthy!

Be Teachable

Unteachable people will never be what they could be. If you are unteachable, you shut yourself off from valuable information whether you know it or not. Many times you feel as though you maybe have attained an advantage over your leader that puts you on their level or above. So what you may be able to preach more eloquently than they can, you don't have the level of influence that they have. So what you feel as though you can teacher more profoundly than your leader, but you may not be able to live what you teach. At all levels, we all can learn something from anyone. Many times you can learn what not to do. The point is if you are teachable, you have the opportunity to find a wealth of knowledge in every situation. Listen to this quote by Michael Jordan:

> "Coming out of high school, I had all the ability in the world but I didn't know the game. Dean (Smith) taught me the game, when to apply speed, how to use your quickness, when to use that first step, or how to apply certain skills in certain situations. I gained all that knowledge so that when I got to the pros, it was just a matter of applying the information. A lot of people say

Dean Smith held me to under 20 points a game. Dean Smith gave me the knowledge to score 37 points a game and that's something people don't understand."

This statement is coming from arguably the best player to ever play the game of basketball. No matter how great he was, he still needed someone to teach the "how" and "when" or the "how not" and "when not". There are great parallels between this instance of sports history and many of our lives. We are operating now with just 20 points per game mentality. If we ever learn to be teachable, we could unlock the potential to do 37 points per game. The ball is really in your court. Often times we fall into this trap because we lose sight of who is really in control anyway. If you keep in perspective that God is the one who gives us pastors after his heart then you understand that it is His will for you to follow someone and be taught. Whenever you refuse to be taught, you are in essence omitting God from the equation. Ken Blanchard says that you will develop an E.G.O. problem. It means that you have Edged God Out:

"We all have been in the presence of and have sometimes even imitated someone who is at least temporarily obsessed with this or her own self-importance. Self-important leaders fill the air with "I," "my," and "me" statements as they enumerate their trials, triumphs and opinions. They are highly sensitive to any criticism or any effort to wrench the spotlight and the microphone from their hands. If there is any credit to be taken for a success or for being right on any subject, they are the first and the last to speak on the subject. What on the surface looks like prideful self-promotion is probably an expression of a more basic sense of at-risk self-esteem and security" (Hodges).

Very simply put, it is beneficial for you to be teachable. It would prove to be an asset to your personal ministry and also an avenue for personal growth in you!

Be Trainable

The worst thing you can say to your leader when asked to do something is, "let me get back to you" or "let me pray about it". Pray about what? This is what you have been called to do. Be flexible. Be pliable. You leader wants to know that they can use you in times of need. This also means that in order to be used you will have to be prepared. You can't allow fear to impede on your progress. Some of us simply will not be thrust into training type situations because it makes us pray harder, study harder, or work harder. Maxwell encourages us even further as he gives us insight to what the fear of failure does to our progress:
1. Paralysis- For some people the fear of failure brings about absolute paralysis. They stop trying to do anything that might lead to failure.
2. Procrastination- steals a person's time, productivity, and potential.
3. Purposelessness- self-pity, excuses misused energy, hopelessness.
(Maxwell, Failing Forward)

When you become untrainable you miss out on valuable experiences. If you are not careful you can say yes to teaching and no to training. You can show up to all of the classroom situations but when it is time to go into the field and apply, you shy away from the experience. If you are going to be effective at all; jump out there and fall, get bruised up, and make mistakes. If you have a 3T leader you will learn how to bandage up your wounds and get back to it. Be Trainable!

Be Trustworthy

One of my favorite bible characters was Joseph. I love the story of Joseph and especially the episode that Joseph had with his leader's wife. This whole situation was a situation of trust. Read this passage with me:

"And Joseph was brought down to Egypt; and Potiphar, an officer of Pharaoh's, the captain of the guard, an Egyptian, bought him of the hand of the Ishmaelite's, that had brought him down thither. (2) And Jehovah was with Joseph, and he was a prosperous man; and he was in the house of his master the Egyptian. (3) And his master saw that Jehovah was with him, and that Jehovah made all that he did to prosper in his hand. (4) And Joseph found favor in his sight, and he ministered unto him: and he made him overseer over his house, and all that he had he put into his hand. (5) And it came to pass from the time that he made him overseer in his house, and over all that he had, that Jehovah blessed the Egyptian's house for Joseph's sake; and the blessing of Jehovah was upon all that he had, in the house and in the field. (6) And he left all that he had in Joseph's hand; and he knew not aught that was with him, save the bread which he did eat. And Joseph was comely, and well-favored. (7) And it came to pass after these things, that his master's wife cast her eyes upon Joseph; and she said, Lie with me. (8) But he refused, and said unto his master's wife, Behold, my master knoweth not what is with me in the house, and he hath put all that he hath into my hand: (9) he is not greater in this house than I; neither hath he kept back anything from me but thee, because thou art his wife: how then can I do this great wickedness, and sin against God? (10) And it came to pass, as she spake to Joseph day by day, that he hearkened not unto her, to lie by her, or to be with her. (11) And it came to pass about this time that he went into the house to do his work; and there was none of the men of the house there within. (12) And she caught him by his garment, saying, Lie with me: and he left his garment in her hand, and fled, and got him out" (Genesis 39:1-12).

I know that is quite a bit of reading but I wanted you to see how Joseph ended up as the illustrious prince of Egypt. He was not command but he was second in command. He was what K. Edward Copeland calls, "Riding in the Second Chariot"

(Copeland). What a level of trust Potiphar had in Joseph. He had given him the authority of his estate and access to his estate all because he trusted him. Joseph had already proven himself to be trustworthy and that is why the king elevated him. Even again, as this story develops the trustworthiness of Joseph shined through the shade of Potiphar's wife's deceit. Even when he had the opportunity to lose his leader's trust, he did not sin against God nor betray his leader. When your leader entrusts you with the vision of the ministry or any assignment to be managed the question you should answer is "Am I worthy of this trust"? Please believe that any training or opportunity you are afforded is not owed to you nor does the leader has to give it. It means they are trying to trust you, so please don't mess it up! A 3T leader will trust you but the question is, are you Trustworthy?

Bibliography

Anthony, Michael J. (1992). *Foundations of Ministry, An introduction to Christian Education for a New Generation*. Grand Rhapids: Baker Books.

Blackaby, Henry and Richard. (2001). *Spiritual Leadership*. Nashville: Broadman & Homan Publishers.

Bruce, Alexander Balmain. (1979). *The Training of the Twelve*. New Caanan, Connecticut: Keats Publishing, Inc.

Chand, Samuel R. *Cracking Your Church's Culture Code*. San Francisco: Jossey-Bass, 2011.

Chand, Samuel R. (2008). *Planning Your Succession*. Highland Park, Illinois: Mall Publishing Co.

Copeland, K. Edward. (2004). *Riding in the Second Chariot*. Rockford: Prayer Closet Publishing.

Edersheim, Alfred. (1993). *The Life and the Times of Jesus the Messiah*. United States: Hendrickson Publishers, Inc.

Henrichsen, Walter A. (1988). *Disciples are Made not Born*. Wheaton: Tyndale House Publishers.

Hewitt, Arthur Wentworth. (1941). *God's Back Pasture, A book of the Rural Parish*. Chicago: The Plimpton Press.

Hodges, Phil & Blanchard, Ken. (1999). *Lead Like Jesus.* Nashville: W Publishing Group, A Division of Thomas Nelson Inc.

Maxwell, John C. (2000). *Failing Forward.* Nashville, TN: Thomas Nelson.

Maxwell, John C. (2007). *Talent is Never Enough Workbook.* Nashville: Thomas Nelson, Inc.

Maxwell, John C. (2003). *The 17 Indisputable Laws of Teamwork, Workbook.* Nashville: Thomas Nelson, Inc.

Maxwell, John C. (2003). *Thinking for A Change.* New York: Time Warner Book Group.

Richards-Bredfeldt, Lawrence O. (1998). *Creative Bible Teaching.* Chicago: Moody Press.

Rogers, Buck. (1987). *Getting the Best out of Yourself and Others.* New York: Harper and Row Publisher.

Rovell, Darren. *Sometimes I dream.* 9 January 2011 http://www.authorviews.com/authors/rovell/rovell-obd.htm

Schwartz, David Joseph. (1959). *The Magic of Thinking Big.* New York: Printice-Hall.

Tidwell, Charles A. (1985). *Church Administration.* Nashville: Broadman & Holman Publishers.

Toler, Stan & Nelson, Alan. (2002). *The 5 Secrets to Becoming a Leader.* Ventura: Regal Books.

Wallace, Curtis. (2011). *The Leadership Gap.* Shippensburg, PA: Destiny Image Publishers, Inc.

Wallace, Curtis. (2011). *The Leadership Gap*. Shippensburg: Destiny Image.

Word Search Corp. (2007). *Holy Bible, American Standard Version*. Austin, TX.

Word Search, Inc. *Strongs Talking Hebrew & Greek Dictionary*. n.d.